THE GRIZZLY BEAR

BY LISA OWINGS

BELLWETHER MEDIA • MINNEAPOLIS, MN

Jump into the cockpit and take flight with Pilot Books. Your journey will take you on high-energy adventures as you learn about all that is wild, weird, fascinating, and fun!

This edition first published in 2012 by Bellwether Media, Inc.

No part of this publication may be reproduced in whole or in part without written permission of the publisher. For information regarding permission, write to Bellwether Media, Inc., Attention: Permissions Department, 5357 Penn Avenue South, Minneapolis, MN 55419.

Library of Congress Cataloging-in-Publication Data

Owings, Lisa.
  The grizzly bear / by Lisa Owings.
    p. cm. – (Pilot books. Nature's deadliest)
  Includes bibliographical references and index.
  Summary: "Fascinating images accompany information about the grizzly bear. The combination of high-interest subject matter and narrative text is intended for students in grades 3 through 7"–Provided by publisher.
  ISBN 978-1-60014-742-5 (hardcover : alk. paper)
  1. Grizzly bear–Juvenile literature. I. Title.
  QL737.C27O97 2012
  599.784–dc23   2011032701

Printed in the United States of America, North Mankato, MN.

010112   1204

CONTENTS

A Grizzly Encounter_____4

A Powerful Predator_____10

Grizzly Bear Attacks_____16

Glossary_____22

To Learn More_____23

Index_____24

A Grizzly Encounter

Jenna Otter was hiking in front of her dad on a steep mountain trail. Her dad had brought her to Glacier National Park in Montana to celebrate her high school graduation. As she rounded a sharp turn, she suddenly found herself face-to-face with a grizzly bear and its cubs.

Johan Otter saw his daughter run past him. Then he saw the bear. It was charging at him with its mouth wide open. The grizzly sank its teeth into Johan's thigh and jerked him from side to side. Johan yelled to Jenna to hide. Then he threw himself 30 feet (9 meters) down the side of the mountain. He wanted to lure the bear away from his daughter. The bear ran after him.

The 400-pound (180-kilogram) grizzly landed on top of Johan. It lifted him by his backpack and shook him violently. Johan fought to escape. The struggle caused him and the bear to tumble farther down the mountain.

Johan grabbed the grizzly's throat and pushed as hard as he could. But he couldn't stop the angry bear. It lunged for Johan's head and clamped its jaws around his skull. Johan could feel his scalp tearing away. He could hear his bones breaking. He knew he was close to death, but he couldn't give up. Jenna was still out there.

Chomp!
A grizzly bear's bite is strong enough to crush a bowling ball!

Johan gathered the last of his strength. He hurled himself once again down the mountain. He landed in a **crevice** too small for the bear to enter. The bear turned to leave. Then Johan heard his daughter scream.

The grizzly **mauled** Jenna's head, shoulder, and back with its teeth and claws. It slit open the side of her mouth. Jenna knew her best chance to survive was to play dead. It worked. The grizzly bear moved on. The bear had been protecting her young, just as Jenna's father had tried to protect her. Johan called out to Jenna. They both had serious injuries, but they were alive.

After the Attack

Jenna Otter and her dad are both doing well after a long and difficult recovery. Johan Otter had to wear a steel halo for three months while his broken neck healed. Jenna was left with a scar from the corner of her mouth to her chin. The two returned to Glacier National Park in 2008 to finish the hike they started three years earlier.

A Powerful Predator

The grizzly bear, one of the most feared animals in North America, is a type of brown bear. It is one of the largest predators on Earth. Male grizzly bears can weigh more than 1,000 pounds (450 kilograms). Some grizzlies tower up to 10 feet (3 meters) tall when standing on their hind legs.

A grizzly's large size doesn't slow it down. Some female grizzlies have been recorded at speeds of 40 miles (64 kilometers) per hour. A person has no hope of outrunning an angry grizzly.

grizzly bear　　**human**

Bear Claws

A grizzly bear's claws can grow up to 4 inches (10 centimeters) long. That's about as long as a human finger!

Grizzly bears are **omnivores**. They eat plants, berries, insects, and fish. They also eat **carrion**. The bears can find food from miles away with their sharp sense of smell. Grizzlies can also smell nuts that squirrels have hidden deep underground. They dig up the nuts with their long claws.

Grizzly bears often steal food from other animals. A single grizzly can scare off an entire pack of wolves and take their kill for itself. Some bears also kill live prey. Any animal that disturbs a hungry grizzly is in danger.

A Super Smeller

A grizzly bear's sense of smell is about seven times better than a bloodhound's.

Garbage-Eating Grizzlies

Garbage at campsites is an easy source of food for grizzlies. However, it brings the bears into contact with humans. These bears are more likely to attack.

Male grizzly bears are ferocious. They battle one another over favorite feeding and fishing areas. They also compete for female bears. The bears roar and slash each other with their front claws. They clamp their jaws around each other's necks and **muzzles**. In some cases, it is a fight to the death.

Though the male grizzly is strong and powerful, the mother grizzly is even deadlier. Female grizzly bears with cubs are responsible for about 8 out of every 10 violent attacks on humans. Grizzly mothers will do anything to protect their cubs. They will take down humans, male bears, or anything else that poses a threat.

Ice Bears

Most grizzly bears sleep through the winter. Some wake up in the middle of winter to look for food. Their fur often gets wet and freezes. Native peoples once feared these "ice bears." They believed no weapon could pierce through the grizzly's armor of ice.

Grizzly Bear Attacks

Grizzly bears are common in Alaska, northwestern Canada, and Glacier and Yellowstone National Parks. These are popular destinations for campers and hikers. Anyone traveling through bear country should take precautions to prevent an attack. Never travel alone through bear country, and do not hike at dawn or dusk. This is when grizzlies **forage** for food.

The best way to avoid a grizzly attack is to be aware of your surroundings at all times. Keep an eye out for bear tracks as you hike, and make noise so you do not surprise a bear. Be careful never to carry smelly food with you. It will attract bears. Bring **bear spray** to use if a grizzly charges.

grizzly bear territory = ☐

bear spray

If you encounter a grizzly bear, try to get out of the way without being noticed. If the bear sees you, stay where you are. Do not run! Avoid eye contact and look off to one side. This imitates **submissive** grizzly body language. The bear may leave you alone if it doesn't think you are a threat.

Limb From Limb

Climbing a tree won't save you from a grizzly bear. They can reach up to 10 feet (3 meters) into the tree. Some grizzlies will even climb up after you!

However, if the grizzly comes toward you with its head and ears lowered, it may charge. Back away slowly. Do not look the bear in the eyes. If the bear attacks, protect your head with your arms and play dead. You will not win a fight with a bear!

Grizzly bears may be deadly, but they also help their environment. They spread berry seeds, and their droppings act as **fertilizer** that helps plants grow. All the digging they do helps keep the soil healthy. Grizzly bears also leave leftover food that other animals can eat.

Grizzly bears are in danger of disappearing. People are hunting them illegally, and **climate change** is making it harder for the bears to find food. It is important that we keep grizzlies safe from **extinction**. At the same time, we must know how to protect ourselves from this fearsome predator. The more we learn about grizzly bears, the better we can prevent attacks and enjoy the North American wilderness.

Attack Facts

- There have been approximately 80 deaths by grizzly bear attacks in the last one hundred years. More than 50 of the deaths were by females defending their cubs.

- Two hikers were killed by grizzly bears in Yellowstone National Park in the summer of 2011. These were the first fatal bear attacks in the park since 1986.

- Yellowstone National Park reports about one bear-caused injury for every 3 million visitors.

Glossary

bear spray—a spray that can sting a bear's eyes; hikers carry bear spray to use if attacked.

carrion—the flesh of dead animals

climate change—any long-term weather change in an area

crevice—a narrow opening in a rock

extinction—when all members of a species have died

fertilizer—a substance added to soil that helps plants grow

forage—to search or hunt

mauled—injured with deep wounds

muzzles—the noses and mouths of some animals

omnivores—animals that eat both plants and other animals

submissive—giving in to or obeying others

To Learn More

At the Library

Sartore, Joel. *Face to Face with Grizzlies*. Washington, D.C.: National Geographic, 2007.

Shapira, Amy, and Douglas H. Chadwick. *Growing Up Grizzly: The True Story of Baylee and Her Cubs*. Guilford, Conn.: Falcon Guide, 2007.

Shea, Therese. *Grizzly Bears*. New York, N.Y.: Gareth Stevens Pub., 2011.

On the Web

Learning more about grizzly bears
is as easy as 1, 2, 3.

1. Go to www.factsurfer.com.

2. Enter "grizzly bears" into the search box.

3. Click the "Surf" button and you will see a list of related Web sites.

With factsurfer.com, finding more information
is just a click away.

Index

Alaska, 16
attack facts, 20
attacks, 4, 7, 9, 13, 15, 16, 19, 20
bear spray, 16, 17
bite, 7
Canada, 16
charging, 4, 19
claws, 9, 11, 12, 14
climate change, 20
cubs, 4, 15, 20
diet, 12, 13
extinction, 20
females, 10, 14, 15, 20
garbage, 13
Glacier National Park, 4, 9, 16
hiking, 4, 9, 16, 20
hunting, 20
jaws, 7, 14

males, 14, 15
mauling, 9
Montana, 4
North America, 10, 20
Otter, Jenna, 4, 7, 9
Otter, Johan, 4, 7, 9
prey, 12
safety, 16, 17, 18, 19
size, 7, 10
smell, 12
speed, 10
teeth, 4, 9
territory, 16
Yellowstone National Park, 16, 20

The images in this book are reproduced through the courtesy of: Don Johnston / Age Fotostock, front cover; Wildstock / KimballStock, pp. 4-5; Biosphoto / Sylvain Cordier / Biosphoto, pp. 6-7; Klein-Buhert / KimballStock, p. 8; John Otter, p. 9; Biosphoto / Theo Allofs / Biosphoto, p. 11; Mat Hayward, pp. 12-13; Jim Chargares, pp. 14-15; Jeff Schultz / Photolibrary, pp. 16-17; Minden Pictures / Masterfile, p. 18; Joel Sartore / National Geographic Stock, p. 19; Andy Rouse / Getty Images, p. 21.